UNVEILING

VERONA

ITALY

Your Guide to the City of Love and Beyond

presented by

Discover your journey!

CONTENTS

CONTENTS

CONTENTS

CONTENTS

VERONA

CITY OF LOVE

Welcome to Verona, a charming city in northern Italy, known for its rich history, architectural marvels, and romantic atmosphere. Verona is famously known as the setting for Shakespeare's tragic love story, Romeo and Juliet, and offers an unforgettable experience for travelers.

Verona, a city that is as rich in history as it is in beauty. Set against the backdrop of the picturesque Adige River, Verona has a timeless allure that has inspired countless visitors. From its well-preserved Roman ruins to the romantic streets that inspired Shakespeare's Romeo and Juliet, Verona has something for everyone. In this travel guide, we've gathered all the information you'll need to explore and enjoy this captivating city, including top attractions, hidden gems, parks and gardens, culinary delights, and even day trips to make the most of your stay.

GREETINGS AND RECOMMENDATIONS FROM LOCALS

Benvenuto, dear traveler! Welcome to the enchanting city of Verona, where love and history are woven together like a fine Italian tapestry. As someone who has experienced the magic of Verona firsthand, I'm delighted to help you uncover the hidden gems and experiences that only a true Veronese would know.

Begin your Verona adventure by embracing our customs, exchanging cheerful "buongiorno" greetings, and sharing smiles and kind words with the people you meet as you wander through the cobbled streets.

You may find yourself strolling along the Adige River and discovering the Roman Theater and Archaeological Museum, a lesser-known treasure. Here, you can step back in time and explore ancient ruins while marveling at the breathtaking view of the city from the museum's terrace.

GREETINGS AND RECOMMENDATIONS FROM LOCALS

Consider venturing off the beaten path to the vibrant neighborhood of Borgo Trento. There, you can stumble upon the picturesque Parco delle Colombare, a peaceful oasis hidden away from the bustling city center. The park's winding paths, charming pond, and lush greenery create the perfect setting for a leisurely afternoon stroll.

When hunger calls, explore a local gem, Osteria La Fontanina. Located near the iconic Castelvecchio, this charming eatery serves authentic Veronese cuisine in a warm and welcoming atmosphere. Make sure to sample their risotto all'Amarone, a delightful dish infused with the flavors of the region's famous wine.

As the sun begins to set, take a short trip to the nearby village of San Giorgio di Valpolicella. Here, you'll find an ancient church perched atop a hill, offering a stunning panoramic view of the surrounding vineyards and the shimmering Lake Garda. The village's serene atmosphere and mesmerizing vistas create the perfect backdrop for a memorable evening.

In the historic heart of Verona, visit the lively Piazza delle Erbe at twilight. This bustling market square transforms into a gathering place where friends share laughter and stories over a glass of local wine. Join them, and as you sip your wine, let the magic of Verona sweep you away.

As you explore Verona, remember to savor each moment and let the city's warmth envelop you. We, the locals, are always here to help, eager to share the magic of our beautiful city with you. Buon viaggio, dear traveler, and may your journey be filled with unforgettable memories!

PRACTICAL INFORMATION

Getting Around

Verona has a compact city center, which is easily explored on foot. For longer distances, you can rely on the efficient public transportation system, which includes buses and bicycles. Taxis and ridesharing services are also available in the city.

When to Visit

Verona has a compact city center, which is easily explored on foot. For longer distances, you can rely on the efficient public transportation system, which includes buses and bicycles. Taxis and ridesharing services are also available in the city.

Currency and Payments

The currency in Verona is the Euro (€). Most businesses accept credit cards, but it's a good idea to carry some cash for smaller purchases, especially at local markets or cafes. ATMs are widely available throughout the city.

Language and Etiquette

The official language in Verona is Italian. While many locals speak English, especially in the tourism industry, it's helpful to learn a few basic Italian phrases to communicate with locals. Italians are generally warm and friendly, and polite gestures like saying "please" and "thank you" are appreciated.

I hope this information helps you plan your visit to Verona. Please let me know if you would like more information or if you are ready to continue with the next section of the guide.

USEFUL LINKS AND PHONE NUMBERS

Emergency Services

General Emergency: 112
Police (Carabinieri): 112
Fire Department (Vigili del Fuoco): 115
Medical Emergencies (Pronto Soccorso): 118

Transportation

Verona Airport (Aeroporto di Verona Villafranca): +39 045 809 5666. Website: https://www.aeroportoverona.it/en
Verona Porta Nuova Train Station: +39 045 923 5665. Website: https://www.trenitalia.com/en.html
ATV (Azienda Trasporti Verona): Local bus service. Website: https://www.atv.verona.it/en

Tourist Information

Verona Tourist Information Office: +39 045 806 8680. Website: https://www.tourism.verona.it/en

Museums and Attractions

Arena di Verona: +39 045 800 5151. Website: https://www.arena.it/en
Juliet's House (Casa di Giulietta): +39 045 803 4303. Website: https://www.turismoverona.eu/en/casa-di-giulietta
Castelvecchio Museum: +39 045 806 2611. Website: www.museodicastelvecchio.comune.verona.it
Verona Cathedral (Duomo di Verona): +39 045 800 6120. Website: http://www.cattedralediverona.it/

City Government

Verona Municipality (Comune di Verona): +39 045 807 9111. Website: /www.comune.verona.it

TOP ATTRACTIONS IN VERONA

ARENA DI VERONA

One of the city's most iconic landmarks, the Arena di Verona is a well-preserved Roman amphitheater dating back to the first century AD. The arena can seat up to 30,000 spectators and is now a popular venue for concerts, operas, and other performances.

Useful Tip: Try to catch a show at the arena, particularly during the annual opera festival, for a unique experience.

Website: www.arena.it

CASA DI GIULIETTA

The Casa di Giulietta, or Juliet's House, is a must-visit for fans of Shakespeare's tragic love story, Romeo and Juliet. The house features a famous balcony, and visitors can write love messages on the walls of the courtyard.

Useful Tip: Be prepared for crowds, as this is a popular attraction. Early morning or late afternoon visits are usually less crowded.

Website: www.turismoverona.eu

PIAZZA DELLE ERBE

This lively square, lined with picturesque buildings, is a great place to soak up the atmosphere of Verona. Piazza delle Erbe is filled with cafes, restaurants, and market stalls, making it a perfect spot to relax, shop, and people-watch.

Useful Tip: Enjoy an authentic Italian gelato or an Aperol spritz at one of the many outdoor cafes in the square.

TOP ATTRACTIONS IN VERONA

BASILICA DI SAN ZENO MAGGIORE

The Basilica di San Zeno Maggiore is a stunning example of Romanesque architecture and is considered one of the most beautiful churches in Northern Italy. Inside, you'll find exquisite frescoes and the famed bronze doors depicting biblical scenes.

Useful Tip: Don't miss the beautiful rose window on the church's facade, known as the "Wheel of Fortune."

Website: www.basilicasanzeno.it

TORRE DEI LAMBERTI

At 84 meters tall, the Torre dei Lamberti is the tallest tower in Verona and offers stunning panoramic views of the city. The tower dates back to the 12th century, and visitors can climb the 368 steps or take the elevator to the top.

Useful Tip: The tower can be busy during peak times, so plan your visit early in the morning or later in the afternoon to avoid crowds.

Website: www.comune.verona.it

PONTE PIETRA

Ponte Pietra is Verona's oldest bridge, dating back to the Roman period. Although partially destroyed during World War II, the bridge was faithfully reconstructed using original materials. The bridge offers beautiful views of the city and the River Adige.

Useful Tip: Visit Ponte Pietra at sunset for a stunning view of the bridge and the surrounding cityscape.

HIDDEN GEMS AND LESSER-KNOWN SIGHTS IN VERONA

GIARDINO GIUSTI

This beautiful Renaissance garden is tucked away from the bustling city center and offers a serene retreat for visitors. With terraces, statues, fountains, and a small labyrinth, the Giardino Giusti is a great place to relax and explore.

Useful Tip: Don't miss the panoramic viewpoint at the top of the garden, which offers stunning views of Verona.

Website: www.giardinogiusti.com

SAN FERMO MAGGIORE

San Fermo Maggiore is a lesser-known church in Verona with a fascinating history. It contains the remains of a 4th-century church in its crypt, while the main building dates back to the 11th century. Inside, you'll find beautiful frescoes and intricate woodwork.

Useful Tip: Look for the small chapel dedicated to St. Francis of Assisi, which features a beautiful painting of the saint.

CASTEL SAN PIETRO

Located on a hill overlooking Verona, Castel San Pietro offers a peaceful escape from the city center and panoramic views of Verona. While the current fortress dates back to the 19th century, the site has been home to various fortifications since Roman times.

Useful Tip: Consider taking the funicular to the top of the hill for an easy and enjoyable ride.

PALAZZO DELLA RAGIONE

Located in the heart of Verona, the Palazzo della Ragione is a medieval palace that served as the city's law court and council chamber. Today, it houses an art gallery featuring works from the Veronese school. The courtyard is a peaceful oasis and a lovely spot to relax.

Useful Tip: Don't miss the stunning frescoes on the walls of the palace's courtyard.

Website: padovacultura.padovanet.it

PORTA LEONI

This ancient Roman gate is one of the oldest in Verona, dating back to the 1st century BC. The gate is named after the nearby church of San Leonardo, and although only half of the original structure remains, it is still an impressive testament to Roman engineering.

Useful Tip: Visit the small archaeological area nearby, where you can see the remains of a Roman road and part of the original city walls.

Website: Porta Leoni

PARKS AND GARDENS IN VERONA

PARCO DELL'ADIGE SUD

Parco dell'Adige Sud is a spacious riverside park that follows the curves of the Adige River. It's an ideal spot for a leisurely walk, run, or bike ride, offering a natural escape within the city. The park has playgrounds, picnic areas, and exercise equipment, making it perfect for families and fitness enthusiasts alike.

Useful Tip: Bring a blanket and enjoy a picnic by the river for a relaxing afternoon.

PARCO SIGURTÀ

Located just outside Verona in the town of Valeggio sul Mincio, Parco Sigurtà is a sprawling, award-winning park and garden covering over 600,000 square meters. It features a diverse range of landscapes, including lush gardens, tranquil ponds, and vibrant flower fields. The park is also home to a variety of wildlife, making it an enchanting destination for nature lovers.

Useful Tip: Rent a bike or a golf cart to cover more ground and explore the vast park comfortably.

Website: www.sigurta.it

PARCO DELLE CASCATE

Located near the small town of Molina, Parco delle Cascate offers a natural oasis away from the hustle and bustle of Verona. The park is filled with lush greenery, picturesque waterfalls, and a network of well-marked walking trails. It's a great spot to escape the city heat and enjoy a picnic in nature.

Useful Tip: Check the website for opening hours and entry fees, as they can change depending on the season.

Website: www.parcodellecascate.it

VERONA'S CULINARY SCENE

RISOTTO ALL'AMARONE

This creamy, rich risotto is made with Amarone wine, which is produced in the Valpolicella region near Verona. The dish is a perfect blend of flavors, with the wine's deep fruity notes complementing the creamy rice.
Where to try: Trattoria Al Pompiere

Website: www.alpompiere.com

BIGOLI

LA type of thick spaghetti, bigoli is a Veronese specialty. It's often served with a sauce made from duck, rabbit, or fresh sardines.
Where to try: Osteria Ponte Pietra

Website: www.ristorantepontepietra.it

PASTISSADA DE CAVAL

A traditional Veronese dish, pastissada de caval is a slow-cooked horse meat stew flavored with red wine, onions, and spices. It's usually served with polenta, a soft cornmeal dish.
Where to try: Osteria Sottocosta

VERONA'S CULINARY SCENE

PANDORO

This sweet, star-shaped cake is a holiday favorite and is often enjoyed during Christmas and New Year celebrations. It's dusted with powdered sugar and has a light, fluffy texture.
Where to try: Pasticceria Flego

Website: www.pasticceriaflego.net

WINE TASTING

If you're a wine lover, don't miss the opportunity to visit one of the local wineries for a tasting of Valpolicella or Soave wines. These renowned wines are produced in the region and showcase the best of Veronese winemaking.

SHOPPING IN VERONA

VIA MAZZINI

This bustling pedestrian street is lined with both international and Italian brands, making it the main shopping hub in Verona. You'll find a mix of clothing, accessories, and footwear stores, as well as cafes and gelaterias to recharge during your shopping spree.

PIAZZA DELLE ERBE

This historic square transforms into a lively market during the day. You'll find an array of stalls selling fresh produce, local delicacies, clothing, and souvenirs. Don't forget to haggle to get the best deals!

CORSO PORTA BORSARI

Located near Piazza delle Erbe, this elegant street is home to a number of high-end boutiques and luxury brands. Stroll down the cobblestone street, and you'll find an array of designer clothing, jewelry, and accessories stores.

SHOPPING IN VERONA

VIA CAPPELLO

For artisanal products and unique souvenirs, head to Via Cappello. This charming street is lined with small boutiques and craft shops, where you'll find traditional Veronese items like handmade leather goods, ceramics, and local wines.

LE CORTI VENETE

Located a short drive from the city center, this shopping center is home to more than 80 stores, including popular Italian and international brands. It's a great option for those looking for a more extensive shopping experience or to escape the hustle and bustle of the city.

PARCO NATURA VIVA

Located a short drive from Verona, Parco Natura Viva is a wildlife park that offers a unique opportunity to see and learn about animals from around the world. The park is divided into two main areas - the Safari Park, where you can drive through enclosures to see animals like lions, giraffes, and rhinos, and the Fauna Park, where you can explore on foot and see smaller animals, reptiles, and birds.

Website: www.parconaturaviva.it

EQUESTRIAN CENTER CLUB IL SALTO

For a family day out in the countryside, visit the Equestrian Center Club Il Salto, which offers horseback riding lessons for beginners and more experienced riders. Children can enjoy pony rides and learn about horse care while exploring the beautiful countryside around Verona.

Website: www.sportingclubparadiso.it

GARDALAND

Just a 30-minute drive from Verona, Gardaland is Italy's largest amusement park and a perfect day trip destination for families. With roller coasters, water rides, and attractions for all ages, there's something for everyone to enjoy. The park also has an adjacent SEA LIFE Aquarium with marine life exhibits.

Website: www.gardaland.it

14

FAMILY-FRIENDLY ACTIVITIES IN VERONA

TORRE DEI LAMBERTI

Give your family a bird's-eye view of Verona by climbing the 84-meter-tall Torre dei Lamberti. This medieval tower offers panoramic views of the city, and there's an elevator to make the ascent easier for younger visitors or those who may have mobility issues.

Website: www.comune.verona.it

GIARDINO GIUSTI

Take a leisurely stroll with your family in the Giardino Giusti, one of Italy's finest Renaissance gardens. The peaceful atmosphere, picturesque fountains, and charming hedge mazes offer a perfect setting for a family picnic or simply enjoying the outdoors.

Website: www.giardinogiusti.com

VERONA BY NIGHT

ILLUMINATED MONUMENTS AND EVENING STROLLS

PIAZZA DELLE ERBE

This historic square is beautifully illuminated at night, creating a magical atmosphere for an evening stroll.

Tip: Don't forget to capture a photo of the stunning Madonna Verona Fountain.

CASTELVECCHIO BRIDGE

The medieval Castelvecchio Bridge is a sight to behold when lit up against the night sky.

Tip: Walk across the bridge for stunning views of the Adige River and the surrounding cityscape.

VERONA BY NIGHT

BARS AND PUBS

CAFFÈ FILIPPINI

Located in the heart of Piazza delle Erbe, Caffè Filippini is an iconic bar with a lively atmosphere.

Tip: Grab a seat on the terrace to enjoy a drink while people-watching.

Website: www.caffefilippini.it

OSTERIA DEL BUGIARDO

This cozy wine bar offers an extensive selection of local wines and delicious appetizers.

Tip: Try their signature "Bugiardini" mini sandwiches.

Website: www.osteriadelbugiardo.it

VERONA BY NIGHT

NIGHTCLUBS AND DANCE CLUBS

BERFI'S CLUB

One of Verona's most famous nightclubs, Berfi's Club features live music and DJ sets in a stylish setting.

Tip: Check their website for upcoming events and dress code requirements.

Website: www.berfis.com

ALTER EGO CLUB

This popular club offers a mix of electronic and dance music, attracting a young and energetic crowd.

Tip: Arrive early to avoid long lines at the entrance. Website:

Website: www.facebook.com/alteregoitaly

VERONA BY NIGHT

LATE-NIGHT DINING

PIZZERIA IMPERO

Open until 1 AM, this pizzeria is perfect for a late-night bite.

Tip: Try their signature "Pizza Impero" with tomato, mozzarella, ham, mushrooms, and olives.

Website: www.pizzeriaimpero.it

OSTERIA AI PRETI

This traditional osteria offers a variety of dishes, including pasta, meat, and fish.

Tip: Make a reservation, as seating is limited. Open until midnight.

Website: www.osteriapreti.it

VERONA BY NIGHT

NIGHTLIFE AREAS

PIAZZA DELLE ERBE

This lively square is surrounded by bars, cafes, and restaurants, making it a popular nightlife destination.

Tip: Explore the nearby side streets to discover hidden gems and local favorites.

CORSO PORTA BORSARI

This historic street offers a mix of bars, clubs, and late-night dining options.

Tip: Stroll along the street to find the perfect spot for your taste and mood.

VERONA BY NIGHT

SAFETY TIPS

- Keep emergency contact numbers handy, including local police and your country's embassy.
- Carry a photocopy of your passport and other important documents, leaving the originals in a safe place.
- Be aware of your surroundings and avoid walking alone in poorly lit or unfamiliar areas.
- Use reputable taxi services or ride-sharing apps when traveling at night.
- Drink responsibly and avoid accepting drinks from strangers.

By following these tips and exploring the diverse nighttime offerings in Verona, you'll be sure to have a memorable experience in this enchanting city.

CASTELVECCHIO MUSEUM

Housed in the historic Castelvecchio Castle, this museum features an extensive collection of sculptures, frescoes, and paintings, mainly from the 14th to the 18th century. Key highlights include works by Pisanello, Paolo Veronese, and Tintoretto.

Website: www.italy-museum.com/venice/castelvecchio-museum

CASTELVECCHIO (MUSEUM OF ARCHAEOLOGY)

This museum showcases Verona's rich archaeological history, with artifacts ranging from the prehistoric period to the Middle Ages. The exhibits include Roman sculptures, mosaics, and inscriptions, as well as early Christian and medieval finds.

Website: museodicastelvecchio.comune.verona.it

VERONA ARENA

Known for its annual opera festival, the Verona Arena is one of the best-preserved Roman amphitheaters in the world. Attend a performance or a concert at this remarkable venue to experience its outstanding acoustics and unique atmosphere.

Website: https://www.arena.it/en

ART AND CULTURE IN VERONA

CASTELVECCHIO MUSEUM

Located in the historic Palazzo della Ragione, this modern art gallery houses works by renowned Italian and international artists from the 19th and 20th centuries. The collection includes pieces by Giorgio de Chirico, Renato Guttuso, and Carlo Carrà, among others.

Website: gam.comune.verona.it

TEATRO ROMANO AND ARCHAEOLOGICAL MUSEUM

Overlooking the Adige River, the ancient Roman theater dates back to the 1st century BC. It still hosts performances during the summer months. The adjoining archaeological museum displays artifacts unearthed in and around Verona, including statues, mosaics, and pottery.

Website: www.archeoveneto.it

ARENA DI VERONA

This well-preserved Roman amphitheater, built in the first century, is one of the most iconic structures in Verona. It's still used today for opera performances and other events, providing a unique atmosphere and unforgettable experience.

Website: www.arena.it

CASTELVECCHIO AND PONTE SCALIGERO

Castelvecchio is a 14th-century fortress built by the Scaligeri family, who ruled Verona during the Middle Ages. Today, it houses the Castelvecchio Museum, which displays an extensive collection of medieval and Renaissance art. The adjacent Ponte Scaligero is a stunning example of a fortified bridge, offering picturesque views of the Adige River.

Website: www.archeoveneto.it

BASILICA DI SAN ZENO MAGGIORE

This stunning Romanesque church is dedicated to the city's patron saint, St. Zeno. The church features beautiful frescoes, an ornate bronze door, and the tomb of King Pepin of Italy. Don't miss the stunning Last Judgment triptych by Andrea Mantegna in the main chapel.

Website: www.basilicasanzeno.it

HISTORICAL AND ARCHITECTURAL LANDMARKS IN VERONA

PIAZZA DELLE ERBE

This lively square in the heart of Verona has been the city's main marketplace since Roman times. Surrounded by stunning historic buildings, including the Palazzo Maffei, the Torre dei Lamberti, and the Casa dei Mercanti, Piazza delle Erbe is a great place to soak up the atmosphere and enjoy an authentic Italian espresso or aperitivo.

ARCHE SCALIGERE

Located near the Church of Santa Maria Antica, the Arche Scaligere is a group of Gothic-style funerary monuments dedicated to the Scaligeri family. The ornate tombs are adorned with intricate carvings and are a testament to the artistic skill and craftsmanship of the period.

Explore the rich history and architecture of Verona, as these landmarks provide a unique insight into the city's past and its cultural heritage.

DAY TRIPS FROM VERONA

Verona's central location in Northern Italy makes it an ideal base for day trips to nearby cities and natural attractions. Here are some recommended day trips from Verona:

LAKE GARDA

Just a short drive from Verona Lake Garda is Italy's largest lake and a popular destination for water sports, hiking, and picturesque towns. Visit Sirmione, known for its thermal baths, Scaligero Castle, and the Grotte di Catullo, or explore charming towns like Malcesine and Gardone Riviera.

Travel time: 40 minutes to 1 hour by car or train

VENICE

The enchanting city of Venice, with its canals, gondolas, and historic architecture, is an unmissable day trip from Verona. Explore the famous sites like Piazza San Marco, the Doge's Palace, and the Rialto Bridge, or simply wander the narrow streets and discover hidden gems.

Travel time: 1.5 hours by train

MILAN

Italy's fashion capital, Milan, offers a mix of historic landmarks and modern attractions. Don't miss the iconic Milan Cathedral (Duomo di Milano), the stunning Galleria Vittorio Emanuele II shopping center, and Leonardo da Vinci's masterpiece, The Last Supper.

Travel time: 1.5 hours by train

DAY TRIPS FROM VERONA

DOLOMITES

The Dolomites, a UNESCO World Heritage Site, offer stunning mountain landscapes and outdoor activities such as hiking, skiing, and mountain biking. Visit charming towns like Cortina d'Ampezzo or take the Great Dolomite Road for a scenic drive through the region.

Travel time: 3 hours by car

PADUA

The historic city of Padua is home to beautiful piazzas, churches, and the world-renowned Scrovegni Chapel, featuring Giotto's frescoes. The city is also known for its prestigious university, which boasts alumni such as Galileo Galilei.

Travel time: 1 hour and 30 minutes by train

BOLOGNA

Bologna, a lively university town, is known for its medieval architecture, vibrant food scene, and the oldest university in the Western world. Wander through the portico-lined streets, visit Piazza Maggiore, and indulge in some authentic Italian cuisine.

Travel time: 1 hour and 30 minutes by train

DAY TRIPS FROM VERONA

VICENZA

Vicenza is a UNESCO World Heritage Site renowned for its stunning Palladian architecture. Explore the Palladian Villas, including Villa La Rotonda, and visit the historic Basilica Palladiana and Teatro Olimpico.

Travel time: 45 minutes to 1 hour by train

MANTUA

Mantua, another UNESCO World Heritage Site, is a charming city with a rich history and stunning art. Visit the Palazzo Ducale, Palazzo Te, and the impressive Basilica of Sant'Andrea. Stroll through the cobblestone streets and take in the beautiful piazzas and medieval architecture.

Travel time: 1 hour and 15 minutes by train

BOLOGNA

Trento is a picturesque city set against the backdrop of the Italian Alps, featuring a mix of Italian and Austrian influences. Discover the historic center, visit the 13th-century Buonconsiglio Castle, and explore the MUSE Science Museum.

Travel time: 1 hour and 30 minutes by train

DAY TRIPS FROM VERONA

FERRARA

Ferrara, another UNESCO World Heritage Site, boasts a well-preserved medieval and Renaissance city center. Explore the impressive Castello Estense, the stunning Cathedral of Saint George, and wander the streets of this charming city.

Travel time: 1 hour and 30 minutes by train

BERGAMO

Bergamo, a historic city split into two distinct parts - the lower, more modern city (Città Bassa) and the upper, medieval city (Città Alta) - offers visitors picturesque views, rich history, and charming streets to explore. Take the funicular to Città Alta, walk along the Venetian walls, and visit the stunning Basilica di Santa Maria Maggiore.

Travel time: Approximately 2 hours by train

ROVERETO

Rovereto, a small city surrounded by hills and vineyards, is known for its art, history, and culture. Visit the MART Museum of Modern and Contemporary Art, explore the Italian War History Museum at Castel Rovereto, and take a stroll through the city's historic center.

Travel time: Approximately 1 hour and 15 minutes by train

DAY TRIPS FROM VERONA

SIRMIONE

FSirmione, located on the southern shore of Lake Garda, is a picturesque town known for its thermal baths and historic sites. Explore the impressive Scaligero Castle, visit the ancient Roman villa Grotte di Catullo, and relax on the shores of Lake Garda.

Travel time: Approximately 1 hour by car

MODENA

Modena, a city in the Emilia-Romagna region, is known for its balsamic vinegar, sports cars (Ferrari and Maserati), and the UNESCO World Heritage-listed Modena Cathedral and Piazza Grande. Visit the Enzo Ferrari Museum, sample local delicacies, and explore the historic city center.

Travel time: Approximately 2 hours by train

These additional day trips from Verona offer a diverse range of experiences for travelers, from picturesque towns and lakeside retreats to cities steeped in history, art, and culture. No matter your interests, there is something for everyone in the surrounding region of Verona.

E N D   N O T E

As our journey through Verona comes to an end, we hope this travel guide has provided you with valuable insights to create a memorable experience. With its historical landmarks, vibrant cultural scene, and natural beauty, Verona is truly a city that enchants visitors with its irresistible charm. Whether you are here for a romantic getaway, a family vacation, or a solo adventure, Verona will leave you with unforgettable memories. Buon viaggio, and happy exploring!

Unlock a world of unforgettable experiences with Tailored Travel Guides! As your go-to source for personalized and meticulously crafted travel guides, we ensure that every adventure is uniquely yours. Our team of dedicated travel experts and local insiders design each guide with your preferences, interests, and travel style in mind, providing you with the ultimate customized travel experience.

Embark on your next journey with confidence, knowing that Tailored Travel Guides has got you covered. To explore more exceptional destinations and discover a treasure trove of additional guides, visit www.tailoredtravelguides.com. Happy travels, and here's to a lifetime of remarkable memories!

Thank you for chosing Tailored Travel Guides!

Discover your journey!

Printed in Great Britain
by Amazon

23355840R00023